Otter Pete
Goes Paddling

Water safety and environmental
conservation for young families

Written by Melanie Seiler
Illustrated by Jannatul Ferdaus Kakon

Otter Pete
Goes Paddling

Water safety and environmental conservation for young families

Dedicated to
Pete Kepner and
Ruthie Gordeuk

Otter Pete loves to play outside.
He enjoys the sun, rain, woods, and fields.
This summer Otter Pete wants to explore rivers.
His aunt Ruthie invites Otter Pete for a river trip.

Otter Pete needs to learn about paddling equipment.
Aunt Ruthie explains they will wear lifejackets to help them float.
Otter Pete tries on a helmet and adjusts the straps.
Aunt Ruthie sets out a whistle, bag of rope, and first aid kit.
Otter Pete picks out a good pair of water shoes.

Point to the throw bag of rope, lifejackets, first aid kit, whistle, and helmet.

Otter Pete learns to plan and prepare before paddling.
Aunt Ruthie reviews maps and river details.
Equipment, drinking water, and snacks are carefully packed.

Otter Pete works hard to carry their gear.
It takes time to get ready and team work to lift the raft.

Otter Pete puts the boat on the water and paddles around.
Aunt Ruthie shows him how to turn and paddle straight.
They study the moving water and rocks.
The boat bounces and splashes through the river.

Otter Pete paddles around the rocks and rides over the waves.
It takes strong muscles and paying attention.
The wind gets stronger and the splashes get bigger.
Aunt Ruthie shows Otter Pete how to make strong paddles strokes.
Otter Pete hits a rock and falls into the river.
He keeps his feet up and climbs back into his boat.

Otter Pete finds a beach to take a break.
Aunt Ruthie takes them to a waterfall.
Many other animals enjoy the waterfall and share it with others.
Sometimes trash is left behind and Aunt Ruthie is always quick to pick it up.

Otter Pete and Aunt Ruthie finish their river trip meeting new friends. Everyone paddles together and talks about great river adventures.
The boats bounce down the river waves.
Otter Pete knows it was a lot of work to prepare but sees the rewards in exploring rivers.

Color sheet

River Journal

- [ ] _____
- [ ] _____
- [ ] _____
- [ ] _____
- [ ] _____
- [ ] _____

Safety tip: Otter Pete taps the top of his head to signal he is safe.

Made in United States
Troutdale, OR
06/22/2024

20732634R00017